In Between

April Pulley Sayre with Jeff Sayre

Beach Lane Books • New York London Toronto Sydney New Delhi

BEACH LANE BOOKS
An imprint of Simon & Schuster Children's Publishing Division
1230 Avenue of the Americas, New York, New York 10020
For information about special discounts for bulk purchases, please contact Simon & Schuster Special Sales
at 1-866-506-1949 or business@simonandschuster.com.
The Simon & Schuster Speakers Bureau can bring authors to your live event. For more information or to book an event, contact
the Simon & Schuster Speakers Bureau at 1-866-248-3049 or visit our website at www.simonspeakers.com.
The text for this book was set in QuickRest.
Manufactured in China
1122 SCP
First Edition
10 9 8 7 6 5 4 3 2 1
Library of Congress Cataloging-in-Publication Data
Names: Sayre, April Pulley, author.
Title: In between / April Pulley Sayre.
Description: New York : Beach Lane Books, 2023. | Audience: Ages 0–8 | Audience: Grades K–1 | Summary: "We all go
through awkward phases-even animals! Award-winning author and photographer April Pulley Sayre shines a light on nature's
relatable in-between moments. No longer underwater but not ready to fly, no longer a tadpole but not yet leaping to land. Animals,
just like people, can find themselves stuck in some awkward in-between stages. How do we get out of the in-betweens? We just
have to push on through! Come get a glimpse behind-the-scenes into nature's in-between moments"– Provided by publisher.
Identifiers: LCCN 2022008066 (print) | LCCN 2022008067 (ebook) | ISBN 9781534487819 (hardcover) | ISBN
9781534487826 (ebook)
Subjects: LCSH: Animals—Miscellanea—Juvenile literature.
Classification: LCC QL49 .S23 2023 (print) | LCC QL49 (ebook) | DDC 590—dc23/eng/20220603
LC record available at https://lccn.loc.gov/2022008066
LC ebook record available at https://lccn.loc.gov/2022008067

For anyone walking the uncertain path
between endings and new beginnings
—A. P. S.

Special thanks to all of April's fans, friends, family, colleagues,
publishers, illustrators, booksellers, and teachers for making
it possible for her to do what she loved—sharing her unique
perspective on nature through words and photographs.
—J. S.

Every creature
on Earth
at times
finds
itself

in
between.

In between
boulders.

In between

branches.

In between
blueberry rows.

In between
inside

and outside,

day

and night.

In between
holding tight

go.

letting

and

There are moments
between bites.

In between
playful and fights.

In between
meals.

In between trips.

In between homes.

Awkward,

unsteady,

in between
fills up
with

not yet,

no longer,

almost.

Almost landed,
but not yet.

Almost asleep,
but not yet.

Almost ready,
but not yet
living on one's own.

In between

leaping

and landing.

In between mother

and another.

In between splashers,

neighbors,

nappers,

petals,

stones.

In the meanwhiles
creatures stretch.

Grow stronger.

They practice holding on

a   little

longer—

for upcoming
in betweens.

Not below,
but still half hiding.

Body transformed,
but not yet gliding.

Nice new knees,
but still not leaping

to lands unknown.

Paws may pause.

Eyes may stare.

But creatures lean in.

Breathe.

Prepare.

For it's
only an
in between.